sundance
publishing

LITTLE RED
READERS

M000196844

At the Supermarket

PETER SLOAN &
SHERYL SLOAN

I put the apples
into the
shopping cart.

I put the bread
into the
shopping cart.

I put the ice cream into the shopping cart.

4

I put the chicken
into the
shopping cart.

I put the milk
into the
shopping cart.

I put the bananas
into the
shopping cart.

Mom paid for
the food,
and I pushed the
shopping cart.